WORSTWARD HO

D1428236

From the same publishers

Samuel Beckett

Novels

Dream of Fair to Middling Women (1932)
Murphy (1938)
Watt (1945)
First Love (1945)
Mercier and Camier (1946)
Molloy (1951)*
Malone Dies (1951)*

The Unnamable (1953) *
How It Is (1961)
Company (1980)**
Ill Seen Ill Said (1981)**
Worstward Ho (1983)**
* published together as the Trilogy
** published together as Nohow On

Short Prose

More Pricks than Kicks (1934)
Collected Short Prose (in preparation)
Beckett Shorts (see below)

Poetry

Collected Poems (1930-1978)
Anthology of Mexican Poetry
(translations)

Criticism
Proust & Three Dialogues with Georges Duthuit (1931,1949)
Disjecta (1929-1967)

Beckett Shorts (A collection of 12 short volumes to commemorate the writer's death in 1989)
1. Texts for Nothing (1947-52)
2. Dramatic Works and Dialogues (1938-67)
3. All Strange Away (1963)
4. Worstward Ho (1983)
5. Six Residua (1957-72)
6. For to End Yet Again (1960-75)

7. The Old Tune (1962)
8. First Love (1945)
9. As the Story Was Told
10. Three Novellas (1945-6)
11. Stirrings Still (1986-9)
12. Selected Poems (1930-85)

WORSTWARD HO

Samuel Beckett

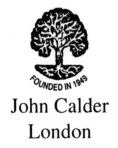

John Calder
London

First Published in Great Britain 1983 by John Calder
Publishers
This edition first published 1999 in Great Britain by
John Calder Publishers
London

© all material in this volume Samuel Beckett Estate 1983, 1999

ISBN 0 7145 40064

British Library Cataloguing in Publication Data
A catalogue record for this title is available from the British
Library

ALL RIGHTS RESERVED

No part of this publication may be reproduced, stored in a retrieval
system, or transmitted in any form by any means, electronic, pho-
tocopying, mechanical or otherwise, except brief extracts for
review, without the prior written permission of the Copyright
owner and publisher

Printed in Canada by Webcom Ltd

WORSTWARD HO

ON. Say on. Be said on. Somehow on. Till nohow on. Said nohow on.

Say for be said. Missaid. From now say for be missaid.

Say a body. Where none. No mind. Where none. That at least. A place. Where none. For the body. To be in. Move in. Out of. Back into. No. No out. No back. Only in. Stay in. On in. Still.

All of old. Nothing else ever. Ever tried. Ever failed. No matter. Try again. Fail again. Fail better.

First the body. No. First the place. No. First both. Now either. Now the other. Sick of the either try the other. Sick of it back sick of the either. So on. Somehow on. Till sick of both. Throw up and go. Where neither. Till sick of there. Throw up and back. The body again. Where none. The place again. Where none. Try again. Fail again. Better again. Or better worse. Fail worse again. Still worse again. Till sick for good. Throw up for good. Go for good. Where neither for good. Good and all.

It stands. What? Yes. Say it stands. Had to up in the end and stand. Say bones. No bones but say bones. Say ground. No ground but say ground. So as to say pain. No mind and pain? Say yes that the bones may pain till no choice but stand. Somehow up and stand. Or better worse remains. Say remains of mind where none to permit of pain. Pain of bones till no choice but up and stand. Somehow up. Somehow stand. Remains of mind where none for the sake of pain. Here of bones. Other examples if needs must. Of pain. Relief from. Change of.

All of old. Nothing else ever. But never so failed. Worse failed. With care never worse failed.

Dim light source unknown. Know minimum. Know nothing no. Too much to hope. At most mere minimum. Meremost minimum.

No choice but stand. Somehow up and stand. Somehow stand. That or groan. The groan so long on its way. No. No groan. Simply pain. Simply up. A time when try how. Try see. Try say. How first it lay. Then somehow knelt. Bit by bit. Then on from there. Bit by bit. Till up at last. Not now. Fail better worse now.

Another. Say another. Head sunk on crippled hands. Vertex vertical. Eyes clenched. Seat of all. Germ of all.

No future in this. Alas yes.

It stands. See in the dim void how at last it stands. In the dim light source unknown. Before the downcast eyes.

Clenched eyes. Staring eyes. Clenched staring eyes.

That shade. Once lying. Now standing. That a body? Yes. Say that a body. Somehow standing. In the dim void.

A place. Where none. A time when try see. Try say. How small. How vast. How if not boundless bounded. Whence the dim. Not now. Know better now. Unknow better now. Know only no out of. No knowing how know only no out of. Into only. Hence another. Another place where none. Whither once whence no return. No. No place but the one. None but the one where none. Whence never once in. Somehow in. Beyondless.

Thenceless there. Thitherless there. Thenceless thitherless there.

Where then but there see—

See for be seen. Misseen. From now see for be misseen.

Where then but there see now—

First back turned the shade astand. In the dim void see first back turned the shade astand. Still.

Where then but there see now another. Bit by bit an old man and child. In the dim void bit by bit an old man and child. Any other would do as ill.

Hand in hand with equal plod they go. In the free hands—no. Free empty hands. Backs turned both bowed with equal plod they go. The child hand raised to reach the holding hand. Hold the old holding hand. Hold and be held. Plod on and never recede. Slowly with never a pause plod on and never recede. Backs turned. Both bowed. Joined by held holding hands. Plod on as one. One shade. Another shade.

Head sunk on crippled hands. Clenched staring eyes. At in the dim void shades. One astand at rest. One old man and child. At rest plodding on. Any others would do as ill. Almost any. Almost as ill.

They fade. Now the one. Now the twain. Now both. Fade back. Now the one. Now the twain. Now both. Fade? No. Sudden go. Sudden back. Now the one. Now the twain. Now both.

Unchanged? Sudden back unchanged? Yes. Say yes. Each time unchanged. Somehow unchanged. Till no. Till say no. Sudden back changed. Somehow changed. Each time somehow changed.

The dim. The void. Gone too? Back too? No. Say no. Never gone. Never back. Till yes. Till say yes. Gone too. Back too. The dim. The void. Now the one. Now the other. Now both. Sudden gone. Sudden back. Unchanged? Sudden back unchanged? Yes. Say yes. Each time

unchanged. Somehow unchanged. Till
no. Till say no. Sudden back changed.
Somehow changed. Each time somehow
changed.

First sudden gone the one. First sudden
back. Unchanged. Say now unchanged.
So far unchanged. Back turned. Head
sunk. Vertex vertical in hat. Cocked back
of black brim alone. Back of black greatcoat cut off midthigh. Kneeling. Better
kneeling. Better worse kneeling. Say now
kneeling. From now kneeling. Could
rise but to its knees. Sudden gone sudden
back unchanged back turned head sunk
dark shade on unseen knees. Still.

Next sudden gone the twain. Next
sudden back. Unchanged. Say now

unchanged. So far unchanged. Backs turned. Heads sunk. Dim hair. Dim white and hair so fair that in that dim light dim white. Black greatcoats to heels. Dim black. Bootheels. Now the two right. Now the two left. As on with equal plod they go. No ground. Plod as on void. Dim hands. Dim white. Two free and two as one. So sudden gone sudden back unchanged as one dark shade plod unreceding on.

The dim. Far and wide the same. High and low. Unchanging. Say now unchanging. Whence no knowing. No saying. Say only such dim light as never. On all. Say a grot in that void. A gulf. Then in that grot or gulf such dimmest light as never. Whence no knowing. No saying.

The void. Unchanging. Say now unchanging. Void were not the one. The twain. So far were not the one and twain. So far.

The void. How try say? How try fail? No try no fail. Say only—

First the bones. On back to them. Preying since first said on foresaid remains. The ground. The pain. No bones. No ground. No pain. Why up unknown. At all costs unknown. If ever down. No choice but up if ever down. Or never down. Forever kneeling. Better forever kneeling. Better worse forever kneeling.

Say from now forever kneeling. So far from now forever kneeling. So far.

The void. Before the staring eyes. Stare where they may. Far and wide. High and low. That narrow field. Know no more. See no more. Say no more. That alone. That little much of void alone.

On back to unsay void can go. Void cannot go. Save dim go. Then all go. All not already gone. Till dim back. Then all back. All not still gone. The one can go. The twain can go. Dim can go. Void cannot go. Save dim go. Then all go.

On back better worse to fail the head said seat of all. Germ of all. All? If of all of it too. Where if not there it too? There

in the sunken head the sunken head.
The hands. The eyes. Shade with the
other shades. In the same dim. The same
narrow void. Before the staring eyes.
Where it too if not there too? Ask not.
No. Ask in vain. Better worse so.

The head. Ask not if it can go. Say no.
Unasking no. It cannot go. Save dim go.
Then all go. Oh dim go. Go for good.
All for good. Good and all.

Whose words? Ask in vain. Or not in
vain if say no knowing. No saying. No
words for him whose words. Him? One.
No words for one whose words. One?
It. No words for it whose words. Better
worse so.

Something not wrong with one. Meaning — meaning! — meaning the kneeling one. From now one for the kneeling one. As from now two for the twain. The as one plodding twain. As from now three for the head. The head as first said missaid. So from now. For to gain time. Time to lose. Gain time to lose. As the soul once. The world once.

Something not wrong with one. Then with two. Then with three. So on. Something not wrong with all. Far from wrong. Far far from wrong.

The words too whosesoever. What room for worse! How almost true they sometimes almost ring! How wanting in inanity! Say the night is young alas and take heart. Or better worse say still a watch of night alas to come. A rest of last watch to come. And take heart.

First one. First try fail better one. Something there badly not wrong. Not that as it is it is not bad. The no face bad. The no hands bad. The no—. Enough. A pox on bad. Mere bad. Way for worse. Pending worse still. First worse. Mere worse. Pending worse still. Add a—. Add? Never. Bow it down. Be it bowed down. Deep down. Head in hat gone. More back gone. Greatcoat cut off higher. Nothing from pelvis down. Nothing but bowed back. Topless baseless hindtrunk. Dim black. On unseen knees. In the dim void. Better worse so. Pending worse still.

Next try fail better two. The twain. Bad as it is as it is. Bad the no—

First back on to three. Not yet to try worsen. Simply be there again. There in that head in that head. Be it again. That head in that head. Clenched eyes clamped to it alone. Alone? No. Too. To it too. The sunken skull. The crippled hands. Clenched staring eyes. Clenched eyes clamped to clenched staring eyes. Be that shade again. In that shade again. With the other shades. Worsening shades. In the dim void.

Next—

First how all at once. In that stare. The worsened one. The worsening two.

And what yet to worsen. To try worsen. Itself. The dim. The void. All at once in that stare. Clenched eyes clamped to all.

Next two. From bad to worsen. Try worsen. From merely bad. Add—. Add? Never. The boots. Better worse bootless. Bare heels. Now the two right. Now the two left. Left right left right on. Barefoot unreceding on. Better worse so. A little better worse than nothing so.

Next the so-said seat and germ of all. Those hands! That head! That near true ring! Away. Full face from now. No hands. No face. Skull and stare alone. Scene and seer of all.

On. Stare on. Say on. Be on. Somehow on. Anyhow on. Till dim gone. At long last gone. All at long last gone. For bad and all. For poor best worse and all.

Dim whence unknown. At all costs unknown. Unchanging. Say now unchanging. Far and wide. High and low. Say a pipe in that void. A tube. Sealed. Then in that pipe or tube that selfsame dim. Old dim. When ever what else? Where all always to be seen. Of the nothing to be seen. Dimly seen. Nothing ever unseen. Of the nothing to be seen. Dimly seen. Worsen that?

Next the so-said void. The so-missaid. That narrow field. Rife with shades. Well

so-missaid. Shade-ridden void. How
better worse so-missay?

Add others. Add? Never. Till if needs
must. Nothing to those so far. Dimly so
far. Them only lessen. But with them as
they lessen others. As they worsen. If
needs must. Others to lessen. To worsen.
Till dim go. At long last go. For worst
and all.

On. Somehow on. Anyhow on. Say
all gone. So on. In the skull all gone.
All? No. All cannot go. Till dim go. Say
then but the two gone. In the skull one
and two gone. From the void. From the
stare. In the skull all save the skull gone.
The stare. Alone in the dim void. Alone
to be seen. Dimly seen. In the skull the

skull alone to be seen. The staring eyes. Dimly seen. By the staring eyes. The others gone. Long sudden gone. Then sudden back. Unchanged. Say now unchanged. First one. Then two. Or first two. Then one. Or together. Then all again together. The bowed back. The plodding twain. The skull. The stare. All back in the skull together. Unchanged. Stare clamped to all. In the dim void.

The eyes. Time to—

First on back to unsay dim can go. Somehow on back. Dim cannot go. Dim to go must go for good. True then dim can go. If but for good. One can go not for good. Two too. Three no if not for good. With dim gone for good. Void

no if not for good. With all gone
for good. Dim can worsen. Somehow
worsen. Go no. If not for good.

The eyes. Time to try worsen. Some-
how try worsen. Unclench. Say staring
open. All white and pupil. Dim white.
White? No. All pupil. Dim black holes.
Unwavering gaping. Be they so said.
With worsening words. From now so.
Better than nothing so bettered for the
worse.

Still dim still on. So long as still dim
still somehow on. Anyhow on. With
worsening words. Worsening stare. For
the nothing to be seen. At the nothing to
be seen. Dimly seen. As now by way of
somehow on where in the nowhere all

together? All three together. Where there all three as last worse seen? Bowed back alone. Barefoot plodding twain. Skull and lidless stare. Where in the narrow vast? Say only vasts apart. In that narrow void vasts of void apart. Worse better later.

What when words gone? None for what then. But say by way of somehow on somehow with sight to do. With less of sight. Still dim and yet—. No. Nohow so on. Say better worse words gone when nohow on. Still dim and nohow on. All seen and nohow on. What words for what then? None for what then. No words for what when words gone. For what when nohow on. Somehow nohow on.

Worsening words whose unknown. Whence unknown. At all costs unknown. Now for to say as worst they may only they only they. Dim void shades all they. Nothing save what they say. Somehow say. Nothing save they. What they say. Whosesoever whencesoever say. As worst they may fail ever worse to say.

Remains of mind then still. Enough still. Somewhose somewhere somehow enough still. No mind and words? Even such words. So enough still. Just enough still to joy. Joy! Just enough still to joy that only they. Only!

Enough still not to know. Not to know what they say. Not to know what it is the words it says say. Says? Secretes. Say better worse secretes. What it is the words it secretes say. What the so-said void. The so-said dim. The so-said shades. The so-said seat and germ of all. Enough to know no knowing. No knowing what it is the words it secretes say. No saying. No saying what it all is they somehow say.

That said on back to try worse say the plodding twain. Preying since last worse said on foresaid remains. But what not on them preying? What seen? What said? What of all seen and said not on them preying? True. True! And yet say worst perhaps worst of all the old man and child. That shade as last worse seen. Left right left right barefoot unreceding on. They then the words. Back to them now

for want of better on and better fail.
Worser fail that perhaps of all the least.
Least worse failed of all the worse failed
shades. Less worse than the bowed back
alone. The skull and lidless stare. Though
they too for worse. But what not for
worse. True. True! And yet say first the
worst perhaps worst of all the old man
and child. Worst in need of worse.
Worst in—

Blanks for nohow on. How long?
Blanks how long till somehow on? Again
somehow on. All gone when nohow on.
Time gone when nohow on.

Worse less. By no stretch more. Worse
for want of better less. Less best. No.
Naught best. Best worse. No. Not best

worse. Naught not best worse. Less best worse. No. Least. Least best worse. Least never to be naught. Never to naught be brought. Never by naught be nulled. Unnullable least. Say that best worst. With leastening words say least best worse. For want of worser worst. Unlessenable least best worse.

The twain. The hands. Held holding hands. That almost ring! As when first said on crippled hands the head. Crippled hands! They there then the words. Here now held holding. As when first said. Ununsaid when worse said. Away. Held holding hands!

The empty too. Away. No hands in the—. No. Save for worse to say. Somehow worse somehow to say. Say for now still seen. Dimly seen. Dim white. Two dim white empty hands. In the dim void.

So leastward on. So long as dim still. Dim undimmed. Or dimmed to dimmer still. To dimmost dim. Leastmost in dimmost dim. Utmost dim. Leastmost in utmost dim. Unworsenable worst.

What words for what then? How almost they still ring. As somehow from some soft of mind they ooze. From it in it ooze. How all but uninane. To last unlessenable least how loath to leasten. For then in utmost dim to unutter leastmost all.

So little worse the old man and child.

Gone held holding hands they plod apart. Left right barefoot unreceding on. Not worsen yet the rift. Save for some after nohow somehow worser on.

On back to unsay clamped to all the stare. No but from now to now this and now that. As now from worsened twain to next for worse alone. To skull and stare alone. Of the two worse in want the skull preying since unsunk. Now say the fore alone. No dome. Temple to temple alone. Clamped to it and stare alone the stare. Bowed back alone and twain blurs in the void. So better than nothing worse shade three from now.

Somehow again on back to the bowed back alone. Nothing to show a woman's and yet a woman's. Oozed from softening soft the word woman's. The words old woman's. The words nothing to show bowed back alone a woman's and yet a woman's. So better worse from now that shade a woman's. An old woman's.

Next fail see say how dim undimmed to worsen. How nohow save to dimmer still. But but a shade so as when after nohow somehow on to dimmer still. Till dimmost dim. Best bad worse of all. Save somehow undimmed worser still.

Ooze on back not to unsay but say again the vasts apart. Say seen again. No worse again. The vasts of void apart. Of all so far missaid the worse missaid. So far. Not till nohow worse missay say

worse missaid. Not till for good nohow
on poor worst missaid.

Longing the so-said mind long lost to
longing. The so-missaid. So far so-missaid. Dint of long longing lost to longing.
Long vain longing. And longing still.
Faintly longing still. Faintly vainly longing still. For fainter still. For faintest.
Faintly vainly longing for the least of
longing. Unlessenable least of longing.
Unstillable vain least of longing still.

Longing that all go. Dim go. Void go.
Longing go. Vain longing that vain
longing go.

Said is missaid. Whenever said said
said missaid. From now said alone. No

more from now now said and now missaid. From now said alone. Said for missaid. For be missaid.

Back is on. Somehow on. From now back alone. No more from now now back and now back on. From now back alone. Back for back on. Back for somehow on.

Back unsay better worse by no stretch more. If more dim less light then better worse more dim. Unsaid then better worse by no stretch more. Better worse may no less than less be more. Better worse what? The say? The said? Same thing. Same nothing. Same all but nothing.

No once. No once in pastless now. No not none. When before worse the shades? The dim before more? When if not once? Onceless alone the void. By no stretch more. By none less. Onceless till no more.

Ooze back try worsen blanks. Those then when nohow on. Unsay then all gone. All not gone. Only nohow on. All not gone and nohow on. All there as now when somehow on. The dim. The void. The shades. Only words gone. Ooze gone. Till ooze again and on. Somehow ooze on.

Preying since last worse the stare. Something there still far so far from wrong. So far far far from wrong. Try better worse another stare when with words

than when not. When somehow than
when nohow. While all seen the same.
No not all seen the same. Seen other. By
the same other stare seen other. When
with words than when not. When somehow than when nohow. How fail say
how other seen?

Less. Less seen. Less seeing. Less seen
and seeing when with words than when
not. When somehow than when nohow.
Stare by words dimmed. Shades dimmed.
Void dimmed. Dim dimmed. All there
as when no words. As when nohow.
Only all dimmed. Till blank again. No
words again. Nohow again. Then all
undimmed. Stare undimmed. That words
had dimmed.

Samuel Beckett

Back unsay shades can go. Go and come again. No. Shades cannot go. Much less come again. Nor bowed old woman's back. Nor old man and child. Nor foreskull and stare. Blur yes. Shades can blur. When stare clamped to one alone. Or somehow words again. Go no nor come again. Till dim if ever go. Never to come again.

Blanks for when words gone. When nohow on. Then all seen as only then. Undimmed. All undimmed that words dim. All so seen unsaid. No ooze then. No trace on soft when from it ooze again. In it ooze again. Ooze alone for seen as seen with ooze. Dimmed. No ooze for seen undimmed. For when nohow on. No ooze for when ooze gone.

Back try worsen twain preying since last worse. Since atwain. Two once so one. From now rift a vast. Vast of void atween. With equal plod still unreceding on. That little better worse. Till words for worser still. Worse words for worser still.

Preying but what not preying? When not preying? Nohow over words again say what then when not preying. Each better worse for naught. No stilling preying. The shades. The dim. The void. All always faintly preying. Worse for naught. Worser for naught. No less than when but bad all always faintly preying. Gnawing.

Gnawing to be gone. Less no good.

Worse no good. Only one good. Gone. Gone for good. Till then gnaw on. All gnaw on. To be gone.

All save void. No. Void too. Unworsenable void. Never less. Never more. Never since first said never unsaid never worse said never not gnawing to be gone.

Say child gone. As good as gone. From the void. From the stare. Void then not that much more? Say old man gone. Old woman gone. As good as gone. Void then not that much more again? No. Void most when almost. Worst when almost. Less then? All shades as good as gone. If then not that much more than that much less then? Less worse then? Enough. A pox on void. Unmoreable unlessable unworseable evermost almost void.

Back to once so-said two as one. Preying ever since not long since last failed worse. Ever since vast atween. Say better worse now all gone save trunks from now. Nothing from pelves down. From napes up. Topless baseless hind-trunks. Legless plodding on. Left right unreceding on.

Stare clamped to stare. Bowed backs blurs in stare clamped to stare. Two black holes. Dim black. In through skull to soft. Out from soft through skull. Agape in unseen face. That the flaw? The want of flaw? Try better worse set in skull. Two black holes in foreskull. Or one. Try better still worse one. One dim black hole mid-foreskull. Into the hell of all. Out from the hell of all. So better than nothing worse say stare from now.

Stare outstared away to old man hind-trunk unreceding on. Try better worse kneeling. Legs gone say better worse kneeling. No more if ever on. Say never. Say never on. Ever kneeling. Legs gone from stare say better worse ever kneeling. Stare away to child and worsen same. Vast void apart old man and child dim shades on unseen knees. One blur. One clear. Dim clear. Now the one. Now the other.

Nothing to show a child and yet a child. A man and yet a man. Old and

yet old. Nothing but ooze how nothing
and yet. One bowed back yet an old
man's. The other yet a child's. A small
child's.

Somehow again and all in stare again.
All at once as once. Better worse all.
The three bowed down. The stare. The
whole narrow void. No blurs. All clear.
Dim clear. Black hole agape on all.
Inletting all. Outletting all.

Nothing and yet a woman. Old and
yet old. On unseen knees. Stooped as
loving memory some old gravestones
stoop. In that old graveyard. Names gone
and when to when. Stoop mute over the
graves of none.

Same stoop for all. Same vasts apart. Such last state. Latest state. Till somehow less in vain. Worse in vain. All gnawing to be naught. Never to be naught.

What were skull to go? As good as go. Into what then black hole? From out what then? What why of all? Better worse so? No. Skull better worse. What left of skull. Of soft. Worst why of all of all. So skull not go. What left of skull not go. Into it still the hole. Into what left of soft. From out what little left.

Enough. Sudden enough. Sudden all far. No move and sudden all far. All least. Three pins. One pinhole. In dimmost dim. Vasts apart. At bounds of boundless void. Whence no farther. Best worse no farther. Nohow less. Nohow worse. Nohow naught. Nohow on.

Said nohow on.